HOW TO FIGHT, LIE, AND CRY YOUR WAY TO POPULARITY

YOUR WAY TO POPULARITY

(and a Prom Date)

First published in 2011 by Zest Books
35 Stillman Street, Suite 121, San Francisco, CA 94107
www.zestbooks.net
Created and produced by Zest Books, San Francisco, CA

Typeset in Nobel
Teen Nonfiction / Humor / Film

Library of Congress Control Number: 2011930949

ISBN: 978-0-9827322-2-9

CREDITS
EDITORIAL DIRECTOR/BOOK EDITOR: Karen Macklin
CREATIVE DIRECTOR: Hallie Warshaw
ART DIRECTOR/COVER DESIGN: Tanya Napier
GRAPHIC DESIGN: Marissa Feind
MANAGING EDITOR/ PRODUCTION EDITOR: Pam McElroy

TEEN ADVISORS: Amelia Alvarez, Ema Barnes, Anna Livia Chen,
Huitzi Herrera-Sobal, and Felicity Massa

Manufactured in China
LEO 10 9 8 7 6 5 4 3 2 1
4500313406

HOW TO FIGHT, LIE, AND CRY YOUR WAY TO POPULARITY
(and a Prom Date)

LOUSY LIFE LESSONS
FROM 50 TEEN MOVIES

Nikki Roddy

Teen movies are awesome. Where else can we see the nerdy girl wind up with the hot school president, the arrogant jerk accidentally fall in love with the girl he's been lying to, or the underdog beat up the school jock and then attain top dog status? We love teen movies because they make us laugh and cry. They give us the opportunity to cheer on our favorite characters as they make their ways through the vicious battlefield of high school. But in the end, what are these movies really teaching us about life?

Let's look at the classic film *Grease*. Sandy finally finds true love with Danny, but not until she ditches her good-girl clothes and gets a slutty makeover. Um, OK. In *Twilight*, Edward woos Bella by telling her he wants to suck all of the blood out of her. That's romantic? In *Carrie*, we learn that teen angst can lead a girl to setting her whole school on fire on prom night (and then killing her mother). And in *Lucas*, the

main character achieves popularity status by throwing himself under a dog pile at a football game. *Dazed and Confused* isn't much better—Sabrina, a freshman girl, becomes popular only after senior girls force her to lie on the ground covered in condiments and flop around like frying bacon.

1976

This stuff is funny, sure, but it's not the kind of behavior you want to base your life on. You don't need to look trampy to get a guy to like you, true love doesn't have to be death defying, and it is not worth sacrificing your life or pride to be popular. Right? There's more to life than fighting, crying, and lying your way to popularity and a prom date. Just maybe not in the movies.

1993

Table of Contents

Rebel Without a Cause

312272
1955

Brooding bad boy Jim just arrived in Los Angeles and he's already making trouble. First, he gets picked up for public drunkenness. Then, he pisses off a popular guy at school, Buzz, by flirting with his girlfriend, Judy. Buzz calls Jim a chicken (the one thing Jim can't stand) and it leads to a knife fight. Jim wins, so Buzz challenges Jim to a game of "chickie run," in which two cars race toward a cliff and the first person to stop is called "chicken." When they play that evening, Jim wins again, but Buzz accidently drives his car off the cliff and dies.

Freaked out, Jim and Judy head to an abandoned mansion to chill out. It's nice and romantic until Plato, Jim's new and slightly crazy friend, shows up to warn Jim that Buzz's friends are out for revenge. Buzz's crew shows up soon after, and Plato starts shooting them (oh, yeah, Plato brought a gun). The cops take Plato down. Plato's death is a bummer, but Jim and Judy still look pretty cute together.

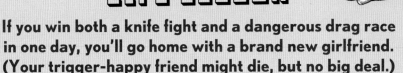

LIFE LESSON

If you win both a knife fight and a dangerous drag race in one day, you'll go home with a brand new girlfriend. (Your trigger-happy friend might die, but no big deal.)

JUDY *[after knowing Jim for one whole day]*: I love you, Jim. I really mean it.

JIM: Well, I'm glad.

Jim (James Dean) defends himself against Buzz (Corey Allen) after Buzz calls him the dreaded "C" word: chicken.

Which of the following common problems does Jim face on his first day at a new school?

a. He's late to homeroom.

b. He can't figure out his locker combination.

c. His new school's cafeteria sucks.

d. He accidently walks into the wrong classroom.

Answer: None of the above. He's too busy playing with knives, cars, and chicks.

Splendor in the Grass 1961

312212

In a small town in 1920s Kansas, Deanie and Bud are in love. But Deanie's mom tells her not to sleep with Bud because girls aren't supposed to enjoy that kind of thing and it would also make her seem "loose." The couple tries to be "good," but Bud eventually cracks from hormone overload. He breaks up with Deanie to fool around with the neighborhood bad girl.

That's when Deanie goes from crazy in love to just plain crazy. She hacks off her hair right before a school dance to look "sexy" and tries to prove to Bud that she, too, can be a bad girl—by desperately offering herself up to him in the parking lot of a school dance. When Bud rejects her advances, she gets hysterical. One of Bud's friends takes advantage of her delirium, and drives her to a local waterfall lookout spot to try and forcefully take advantage of her (she keeps yelling, "Stop, Bud!"). Finally, she breaks free and tries to kill herself by jumping off the waterfall dam. Some onlookers jump in and save her. She lives, but her parents commit her to a mental institution. Bud goes on to become a modest rancher and Deanie gets engaged to a guy from the institution. They see each other again years later, but are left with only memories of their crazy past.

LIFE LESSON

If you take your parents advice and don't have sex with your high school love, you'll get dumped and wind up in a mental institution.

Deanie's Foolproof Steps to Becoming a Bad Girl

1. End fights with your parents by running around the house naked.

2. Give yourself an extreme at-home haircut.

3. Try to awkwardly seduce your ex after he has already dumped you.

4. Wear a slutty dress to the school dance and start smoking cigarettes.

5. Repeat steps 1-4 until desired bad girl status is achieved. Warning: This may lead to being placed in lockdown.

Bud (Warren Beatty) plants a steamy smooch on Deanie (Natalie Wood) before she pushes him away. No kissing for good girls!

SOUND BITE

BUD: Deanie, you're a nice girl.

DEANIE: I'm not. I'm not a nice girl.

Carrie  1976

At Bates High School, Carrie (a.k.a. Creepy Carrie) is the strange, shy girl with hair in her face. She has a mother who tells her that pimples are punishment from God, locks her in a closet to pray, and refuses to teach her about menstrual periods (because they are only "for sinners"). But Carrie does have one gift: She can move things with her mind. And when she gets pissed, she uses telekinetic powers to fling ashtrays across the room and shatter mirrors.

Then, one day in gym class, Carrie finally gets her period (she doesn't know what it is, thanks to her psycho mother), and the popular girls laugh at her and pelt her with tampons. When the gym teacher punishes the mean girls, the awful ringleader, Chris, decides to get revenge on Carrie: Chris rigs the prom queen election so that Carrie will win, and then dumps a bucket of pig's blood on her while she's on stage. That's when Carrie decides it's time to use her telekinetic powers to kill everyone in the gym. After the blood bath is over, Carrie walks home, kills her mother by telekinetically hurling kitchen knives, and then uses her powers to suck the house down into the ground, with her inside.

LIFE LESSON

When girls are bullying you at school, solve the problem by killing them with your telekinetic powers, and then finish the job on your mom.

CARRIE *[after she's just killed everyone at the prom]*: It was bad, Mama. They laughed at me.

Covered in pigs' blood, Carrie (Sissy Spacek) expresses typical teen angst by murdering everyone at the prom, including her prom date, Tommy (William Katt).

Top Five Reasons Carrie Shouldn't Have Sucked Herself Down With the House

1. It's difficult, but not impossible, to get pig's blood out of a prom dress.

2. All of the mean popular kids are dead.

3. A burned down school equals no classes for a little while.

4. Her crazy mom is gone and so is her curfew and locked-in-the-closet time.

5. Telekinetic powers are good for getting away from the police.

Grease  *1978*

On a beach in California, local teen Danny and Australian tourist Sandy meet over the summer and fall in love. After three months of building sand castles and frolicking in the waves, the lovebirds have a tearful goodbye as Sandy prepares to go home. With Sandy gone, Danny starts his senior year at Rydell High School, all set to rule the school with his wild crew of friends, the "T" Birds. Then he finds out that Sandy's family ended up staying in California and she's a new Rydell student. To keep up with his bad boy reputation, Danny acts like a jerk to Sandy, instead of the sweet, romantic boy he was at the beach—and Sandy dumps him.

Devastated, Danny spends the rest of the year wrestling with whether or not he should clean up his image. Eventually, he goes out for track so he can earn a varsity letter to make Sandy proud (and get her back). By the end of the school year, Danny is practically a model citizen. However, Sandy suddenly decides she wants to ditch her wholesome good-girl look for painted-on black spandex pants, curls, and a cigarette. Danny's ecstatic over the new rock 'n' roll Sandy, and the two climb into Danny's car and happily fly off into the sky together. No, seriously. The car flies up into the sky.

LIFE LESSON

To find true love, you need to completely change the things you like, the way you act, and how you dress. (Wearing spandex helps, too.)

Sandy's Tips for Finding True Love

1. Trade all of your flat shoes for unnaturally high heels.

2. Transform pin-straight hair into tiny bouncing curls.

3. Replace all your normal clothing with new, skin-tight duds.

4. Start smoking.

5. Make sure you don't recognize yourself in the mirror; it means you're on the right track for a healthy, long-lasting relationship.

Danny (John Travolta) dances excitedly with the new and "improved" sexpot Sandy (Olivia Newton-John).

SOUND BITE

DANNY *[seeing the new, spandex-clad Sandy]:* Sandy!

SANDY: Tell me about it, stud.

Fast Times at Ridgemont High

1982 312272

Stacy, a high school freshman, spends her time waitressing at a restaurant in the mall and worrying about her inexperience with boys. But according to her friend Linda, dating is easy: You simply go out with any cute mall dude that asks you and practice your oral sex "technique" on a carrot in the lunchroom. Armed with Linda's advice, Stacy goes out with a creepy older guy she meets at her job. He takes her to a deserted baseball dugout where, on their first date, she loses her virginity.

Later in the year, she meets Mark "Rat" Ratner, a sweet and geeky romantic from school, but she scares him off by inviting him over and then changing into her bathrobe at the end of their first date. Rat gets overwhelmed and awkwardly flees the scene. Then, Stacy invites Rat's best friend, Damone, to go swimming after school. And she has sex with him in the pool house—and gets pregnant. Damone is a complete jerk about it, and doesn't even help pay for the abortion. Stacy realizes the virtues of dating nice guys and gets back together with Rat.

LIFE LESSON

To appreciate the nice guy who won't take advantage of you in your bathrobe, get impregnated by his jerk of a best friend.

What is the most important thing Stacy learned her freshman year of high school?

a. The importance of Shakespeare.

b. How to solve advanced algebra equations.

c. Why cafeteria food sucks.

d. How to lie about her age, lose her virginity, get pregnant, and distinguish the losers from the nice guys.

Answer: d. Who learns algebra anymore?

Using carrots, Linda (Phoebe Cates) gives Stacy (Jennifer Jason Leigh) lessons in the school lunchroom on perfecting her sexual technique.

SOUND BITE

STACY: I want a relationship. I want romance.

LINDA: In Ridgemont? We can't even get cable TV here, Stacy, and you want romance.

Valley Girl 1983

Julie Richman is the quintessential Valley Girl. She is addicted to the word "totally," surrounded by the popular crowd, and has the coolest boyfriend in the valley, Tommy. But when he starts treating her "like a piece of furniture," she dumps him, much to the shock of everyone she knows. Then she meets a leather-clad, Hollywood punk kid with a romantic streak, named Randy. They go to punk shows, share sodas, suck face on the Sunset Strip, and fall in love.

But Julie's friends (totally!) don't approve. So she winds up dumping Randy and getting back together with her socially acceptable ex. Randy stalks her repeatedly and then, on the night of the junior prom, sneaks into the prom in a tux jacket, skinny tie, black jeans, and spikey 'do—and kicks the bejesus out of Tommy. Tommy, in his powder-pink tuxedo, still tries to stop Julie from leaving with Randy, but she fights back by smashing guacamole in his face and takes off into the night with her punk-rock loverboy.

LIFE LESSON

Date the obnoxious jock until a hot, renegade punker with a violent streak sweeps you off your feet.

Randy (Nicolas Cage) takes Julie (Deborah Foreman) to a grimy punk club in Hollywood. With her preppy clothes and limited vocabulary, she's just a little out of place.

Randy's Brilliant Tactics for Getting Your Girlfriend Back

1. Slip photo-booth photos of yourself in her school book.

2. Pose as a movie theater worker when she goes to see a movie.

3. Pose as a fast-food worker when she's getting food with the guy she dumped you for.

4. Camp out on her front lawn in a sleeping bag.

5. When 1-4 fails, crash her junior prom and kick her date in the crotch.

Risky Business 1983 312272

Joel is a straight-and-narrow student in a wealthy Chicago suburb with dreams of getting into an Ivy League college. But when his parents leave town for a trip, he decides to spend the week partying with his two favorite, and generally unavailable, things: his dad's Porsche and a hot girl.

He takes the Porsche for a few spins, and hooks up with Lana, a gorgeous and mysterious prostitute. But after their first night together, she steals his mom's expensive crystal egg from the living room. His attempt to retrieve it involves a car chase with Lana's gun-toting pimp, and the Porsche ends up at the bottom of Lake Michigan. Joel should be screwed, but Lana and her fellow call girls help him turn his house into a brothel for a night to get money to fix the car. Unfortunately, Lana's pimp steals all the furniture from his house that night, but Joel manages to buy it back. When his parents return, they are none the wiser. And then Joel gets into Princeton.

LIFE LESSON

If you lie to your parents, steal your dad's car, and solicit a prostitute, you'll get into an Ivy League school.

When should Joel have realized that Lana couldn't be trusted?

a. When he orders her "services" over the phone.

b. After she steals his mom's expensive crystal egg.

c. When she gets him into a car chase with a guy waving a gun.

d. Around the time her pimp robs his house.

Answer: All of the above. (And this guy gets into Princeton?)

Lana (Rebecca De Mornay) refuses to leave Joel's (Tom Cruise) house after spending the night. (She has already stolen his mother's crystal egg, but at least she makes breakfast.)

SOUND BITE

JOEL *[leaving Lana in his house after she's already stolen the crystal egg]*: Don't steal anything. If I come back here and anything's missing, I'm going straight to the police. I mean it.

Lana: Go to school, Joel. Learn something.

Sixteen Candles 1984

312272

It's Sam's 16th birthday and her family doesn't even notice because they're too busy planning her sister's wedding. On top of that, she can't seem to get Jake Ryan, the hottest senior guy in school, to notice her. Jake's girlfriend, Caroline, has a ridiculously hot body and Sam has a tragic lack of curves.

Then, on her birthday, Sam accidentally drops a "sex quiz" in the school hallway. Jake finds it, and sees that his name is written in response to the question asking who Sam wants to "do it" with. Suddenly, Jake is intrigued. As the day goes on, Jake tries to figure out more about Sam, which includes having a heart-to-heart with a geeky freshman named Ted who's in love with Sam. The next day, which happens to be Sam's sister's wedding day, Jake breaks up with Caroline and shows up in front of the church, ready to pick Sam up and make out. Later that night, he even brings her a belated birthday cake.

LIFE LESSON

To snag your dream guy, just let him know you want to "do it" with him.

After Jake finds Sam's sex quiz, he:

a. Brags to his friend about how Sam is "always looking at" him.

b. Threatens to kick Ted's ass if he finds out that Ted lied to him about Sam's affections.

c. Hands his drunk and practically unconscious girlfriend over to Ted, so that Ted could mess around with her.

d. Dumps his girlfriend, using her "hookup" with Ted as an excuse.

Answer: All of the above. Does Jake seem like kind of a creep to anyone else?

On the morning of her sister's wedding, Sam (Molly Ringwald) finds Jake (Michael Schoeffling) outside the church, ready to sweep her off her feet—and maybe find out if she really meant what she said in the sex quiz.

SOUND BITE

JAKE *[leaning over Sam's birthday cake]*: Happy birthday, Samantha. Make a wish.

SAMANTHA: It already came true.

Footloose 1984

In the small town of Beaumont, Texas, public dancing is illegal. This is because Reverend Moore, who lost a son to a drunk driving accident, convinced the town that public dancing leads to immoral behavior. Most of the townspeople go along with it, except for Moore's own daughter, Ariel, whose favorite hobbies include underage drinking, premarital sex in the woods, and wearing the red cowboy boots her father hates.

Enter Ren, a rebellious new kid from Chicago who busts spontaneous acrobatic dance flips when he needs to blow off steam. He loves to dance and teams up with the rebel Ariel to start planning a senior prom. This means having to convince the town that dancing is not a sin. But despite their efforts, which include citing Bible verses in support of dancing at a city council meeting, they can't get the town or the Reverend to budge. Then, in Ren's darkest hour, he finds an old grain mill that just happens to be right outside county lines where dancing is still legal. The dance is on! In the end, the Reverend changes his mind anyway, and the seniors party as confetti inexplicably rains from the ceiling.

LIFE LESSON

If you're not allowed to dance, merely cross the county lines. You'll be forgiven anyway, and rewarded with a party.

With public dancing illegal, the citizens of Beaumont keep themselves busy by:

a. Hassling new high school students.

b. Starting bar brawls with burly cowboys.

c. Racing tractors toward each other to prove who's "chicken."

d. Rallying together for book burnings.

Answer: All of the above. Thank goodness they're not allowed to dance and can focus on more wholesome, productive activities.

To blow off steam, bad boy Ren (Kevin Bacon) smokes a cigarette and dances alone.

SOUND BITE

REVEREND MOORE: If our Lord wasn't testing us, how would you account for the proliferation, these days, of this obscene rock 'n' roll music, with its gospel of easy sexuality and relaxed morality?

A Nightmare on Elm Street

1984
312272

Nancy and her friends are all having nightmares about the same guy: a demented killer with burn scars and a homemade knife glove. The weird thing is, when this psycho slashes them up in their nightmares, they also get slashed up (or even killed) in real life. A few nightmares and three dead friends later, Nancy knows she's in trouble. She sucks back an industrial-size pot of coffee and begins investigating who this murderer might be. She finds out that he (Fred Kruger) was a child killer from the neighborhood when she was a kid. The local parents tracked him down vigilante-style and burned him alive, and now he's getting revenge on those parents' teenagers.

Nancy figures out how to pull Freddie out of her dream, thinking she can kill him that way, but he kills her mother. Then, Nancy realizes that her fear is what gives him power. So she stands up to him and he disappears! The next morning, Nancy awakens to a sunny day with all of her loved ones alive again. Her mother waves her off as she and her friends drive away. Everything is wonderful until the hood of the convertible comes down and traps them all. As they scream, Freddie's arm pulls Nancy's mother by the neck back inside the house. Clearly, Freddy isn't dead.

LIFE LESSON

If you aren't afraid of the psychotic killer, you might be able to conquer him. But maybe not. Good luck with that.

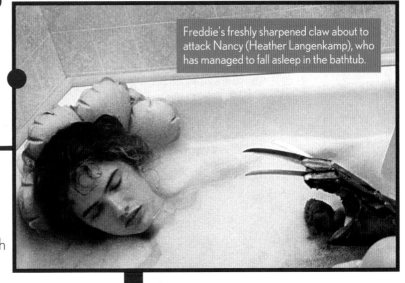
Freddie's freshly sharpened claw about to attack Nancy (Heather Langenkamp), who has managed to fall asleep in the bathtub.

What does Freddie do to Nancy in her nightmares?

a. Melts himself through her ceiling to attack her.

b. Morphs her bathtub into a pool of deep water and attempts to drown her.

c. Licks her with his nasty tongue through the phone.

d. Turns the staircase into goo as she's trying to run away.

Answer: All of the above. Yeah, Nancy doesn't really stand a chance.

The Karate Kid 1984

312272

New Jersey kid Daniel has just moved to Los Angeles, where he is knee-deep in palm trees and rich kids. Not exactly his scene, but things are looking up after he meets Ali, a pretty girl from the hills. That is, until Ali's ex-boyfriend, Johnny—a blonde musclehead hopped up on jealous rage—starts using skinny Daniel as his personal punching bag.

Daniel tries to join the local karate dojo to learn self-defense, but finds out that Johnny is the star student. So instead, he avoids Ali at school, and spends his free time trimming bonsai trees with his apartment building's Chinese maintenance man, Mr. Miyagi, who just happens to be a master of karate. Mr. Miyagi takes Daniel on as a student and makes him paint fences, wax cars, and scrub floors as training. This somehow transforms Daniel into a karate expert. At the end of the movie, Daniel has a face-off with Johnny at a local tournament and despite an injured leg, and the fact that he's still *really* skinny, Daniel wins the fight with an awkward-looking crane kick.

LIFE LESSON

If the school bully is destroying you, ask your building's handyman to train you in martial arts.

Daniel (Ralph Macchio) sands Mr. Miyagi's floors as part of his highly skilled martial arts training.

Rules of Mr. Miyagi's Fail-Proof School of Karate

1. Bond with your student over bonsai tree trimming.

2. Assign your student the annoying household chores you've been putting off forever and call it "training."

3. Sign your student up for a pro-level karate tournament when he's never been in a real fight.

4. Collect the winning trophy.

Teen Wolf 1985

Seventeen-year-old Scott has a fear of being "average," but it seems he's destined for being just that. His high school basketball team sucks and his crush Pamela—star of the school play—ignores him. Then one night during a full moon, something un-average happens to Scott: His fingernails turn into claws and his entire body sprouts a shaggy fur coat. Turns out he's from a family of werewolves, and, from that point forward, he can "wolf out" anytime at will.

At first, he's horrified—what will people think? But people don't seem to care because wolf-Scott can dunk on the basketball court. Suddenly, he is the star basketball player, which equals a school-wide consensus that fur and claws are hot. Even Pamela gets wolf fever and the two hook up (yes, even when he's a wolf.) Unfortunately, wolf-Scott's ego and temper get out of control and his best girl friend Boof (who is also in love with him) encourages him to go back to being the plain ol' human Scott. He takes her advice, but retains his wolfish confidence, popularity, and basketball skills.

LIFE LESSON

To give your confidence, social status, and sports skills a boost, spend some time as a self-obsessed, hyper-aggressive canine.

Scott (Michael J. Fox), as a wolf, surfs atop of his friend's van. He's that cool.

The best thing about becoming a wolf is that it gives Scott the courage to:

a. Break dance in the school hallway.

b. Flirt with Pamela in front of everyone, including Boof.

c. Steal the basketball from his own teammate to make a basket.

d. Surf on top of his friend's van as it tears down the street.

Answer: All of the above. Being an egotistical jerk never felt so good.

The Breakfast Club 1985

312272

Five Illinois high school kids get stuck together for a day of detention: Claire, the spoiled princess who got caught skipping school to go shopping; Andrew, the star jock who got busted for taping some geek's buns together; Brian, the super nerd who's in trouble for a mysterious explosion in his locker; John, the wild delinquent who is always in detention; and Allison, the weird girl who showed up to detention because she had nothing better to do.

In the beginning, they see each other according to the stupid stereotypes that define their high school reputations, but as the day goes on, their defenses come down, and they start having fun. They dance around the library (where Principal Vernon has stuck them). Brian becomes social. Claire gives Allison a makeover, taking her from punk-girl-meets-hobo to generic preppy with frilly blouse. Andrew suddenly notices Allison, now that she's all cleaned up. And Claire and John give in to the awesome feeling of kissing someone you kind of hate, and make out in the janitor's closet. By the end of detention, everyone is friends and doing stuff they thought they'd never do.

LIFE LESSON

With the right mix of stereotypical personalities, a day in detention can become a life-changing experience.

Which of the following pickup lines does John use on Claire?

a. "Would you like to go out on a date?"

b. "Wow, you're really pretty."

c. "I think I'm starting to like you."

d. "Stick to the things you know: shopping, nail polish, your father's BMW, and your poor, rich, drunk mother in the Caribbean."

Answer: d. John knows how to treat a lady.

The group (Molly Ringwald, Anthony Michael Hall, Emilio Estevez, Ally Sheedy, and Judd Nelson) bonds over how crappy it is to be a teenager.

SOUND BITE

CLAIRE *[to John, after he convinces everyone to sneak out of the library to get pot from his locker]:* How do you know where Vernon went?

JOHN: I don't.

CLAIRE: Well, how do you know when he'll be back?

JOHN: I don't. Being bad feels pretty good, huh?

Pretty in Pink 1986

312272

Andie is an artsy high school girl from the wrong side of the tracks. She has friends who love her, and a best friend named Duckie who is *in* love with her, but Andie still can't help falling for the wealthy Blane. Blane actually likes her too and asks her to the prom, but when his rich, snobby friends make fun of Andie's low social status and her flair for making her own clothes, he bails on her. His excuse: He forgot that he already had a prom date. Um, OK.

Devastated but determined to prove that the rich kids didn't break her spirit, Andie hacks apart two perfectly good pink dresses to make her own extra special prom dress and braves the dance alone. That is, until Duckie shows up right before she's about to walk in, and offers to be her date. After they walk in, Blane instantly realizes he's been an idiot, and tells Andie he loves her, which is enough to convince her that he's not a spineless tool anymore. And the ever-loyal, lovesick Duckie unselfishly gives his blessing because that's just what friends do. Right?

LIFE LESSON

Your rich, popular boyfriend may be ashamed of you and dump you right before prom, but as long as he apologizes for it, you'll have a magical night together.

Which of the following does Blane do to prove he's sorry?

a. Gives Andie flowers.

b. Apologizes to her in front of his friends.

c. Writes Andie a poem.

d. Compliments her on her dress.

Duckie (Jon Cryer) takes Andie (Molly Ringwald) to the prom because Blane broke up with her. Duckie doesn't know yet that he won't leave with Andie that night.

SOUND BITE

IONNA *(Andie's friend)*: Love is awful, isn't it?

35

Lucas  1986

312272

Lucas is a sensitive young high school student who's a bit short and a bit awkward and loves bugs. Then over one summer, he befriends Maggie, a pretty new girl in town, and falls for her. But she just likes him as a friend. When school starts, Maggie joins the cheerleading squad (even though Lucas tells her it's beneath her) and grabs the attention of the football player Cappie, an upperclassman guy Lucas has always looked up to. The jealousy, it burns.

So Lucas does what any man in love would do: He ambushes the high school football game by running onto the field in a stolen jersey. He actually almost catches a goal-worthy pass, but drops the ball and ends up unconscious at the bottom of a giant football player dog pile. Not only does he live through it, but he becomes a minor celebrity: When he goes back to school, he finds a varsity football jacket with his name on it in his locker. And the jocks who used to torment him slow clap for him as he walks down the hallway. Maggie, however, is still dating Cappie.

LIFE LESSON

A concussion might not get a girl to like you, but it will amp up your social status.

The next time Lucas wants to get a girl to like him, he should avoid which of the following?

Lucas (Corey Haim) tries to talk with Cappie (Charlie Sheen), but Cappie is too busy flirting with Maggie (Kerri Green).

a. Taking her on a date that involves crawling through the city's sewer system.

b. Insulting her decision to join the cheerleading squad.

c. Introducing her to his older, hotter friend.

d. Removing his helmet when ambushing the football game to impress her.

Answer: All of the above. Lucas is not exactly a romance role model.

Ferris Bueller's Day Off

1986 312272

Ferris Bueller is a teenage legend known for doing whatever he wants and never getting in trouble. So, one spring day, he convinces his neurotic best friend, Cameron, to steal his father's limited edition Ferrari (Cameron's dad loves the car more than he loves Cameron), trick the school principal, pick up Ferris and his girlfriend, Sloane, and spend the day ditching school in downtown Chicago. After dropping the Ferrari off at a parking garage, they go to a baseball game, visit a museum, and eat at a fancy restaurant. Then Ferris leads the town in an impromptu dance atop a street parade float.

But when they return to the car, they find that the parking garage attendants took the Ferrari for a ride, adding hundreds of extra miles to the odometer, which Cameron knows his dad will notice. Ferris convinces him they can get the miles off by propping the car up in Cameron's elevated, glass-wall garage and throwing it into reverse for a while. It doesn't work and the car winds up careening out of the garage, breaking the glass wall, and flying into the trees behind the house. Ferris offers to take the blame for the whole mess. But Cameron insists on taking responsibility, reasoning that it will be an excuse to finally talk to his dad about their relationship issues.

LIFE LESSON

To jumpstart a better relationship with your dad, let your best friend cost him millions in property damage.

Which "faking sick" trick gets Ferris caught?

a. Licking his palms in order to have sickly, clammy hands.

b. Arranging a life-size dummy to take his place in bed.

c. Setting up an audiotape of his own snoring sounds.

d. Hacking into the school's computer system to erase his previous sick days.

Answer: None of the above. Ferris never gets caught. He only gets other people in trouble.

Ferris (Matthew Broderick), Sloane (Mia Sara), and Cameron (Alan Ruck) stare down at the totaled Ferrari, which just flew out of the elevated garage. Oops.

SOUND BITE

CAMERON *[after the car has flown out of the garage]*: What'd I do?

FERRIS: You killed the car.

License to Drive 1988

Sixteen-year-old Les knows that a license is his ticket to freedom and a date with Mercedes, a curly-haired teen vixen who likes guys who drive. But he fails the written portion of the driver's test. So, when Mercedes calls Les to go on a date, he decides to—what else?—steal his grandfather's expensive Cadillac to take her out.

He takes Mercedes to a nightclub, where she chugs a bottle of champagne. Afterward, she dances on the Cadillac with her heels, denting the hood. Then she passes out. Les throws her into the backseat and heads to his friend Dean's house to bang out the dents. After that, Les, Dean, another friend Charles, and Mercedes (still unconscious) take a joyride, which includes barreling through a fence, driving through a mob of military protesters, and temporarily losing the car to a crazy drunk guy. By the next morning, the car is destroyed (and only drives in reverse). But Les doesn't get in trouble because his pregnant mother is in labor and his parents need a ride to the hospital. Les takes them, tearing down the road backwards and almost killing several pedestrians—but his folks are happy for the ride. Meanwhile, Mercedes agrees to a second date. And she lets Les drive her car.

LIFE LESSON

Become an illegal and reckless driver, and you'll win the respect of your parents and score a girlfriend.

LES *[to his dad]:*
You know, I don't need the BMW any-more ... *[Mercedes pulls up and honks the horn]* I already have a Mercedes.

Les' dad (Richard Masur) is pissed that Les (Corey Haim) failed his driver's test. He doesn't know yet that Les is going to steal and total the Cadillac.

Les thinks Mercedes is a special girl because she is:

a. Fun. She loves getting wasted and dancing on cars.

b. Easygoing. She doesn't mind riding around with him and his friends all night (albeit, she's unconscious, but still).

c. A cheap date. She doesn't cost him anything after she passes out.

d. Generous. She lets her boyfriend drive her car, after all.

Answer: All of the above. She's a catch!

Heathers 1988

312272

Veronica is a popular girl at Westerberg High and her friends (Heather D., Heather M., and Heather C.) make up the most exclusive clique in school: The Heathers. But Veronica hates the ruthless leader of the clan, Heather C., and is starting to regret sacrificing her soul at the altar of popularity. To rebel, she starts dating J.D., a new bad boy at school with a burning hatred for high school cliques. They're a match made in teen angst heaven.

Then one day, J.D. and Veronica joke about killing Heather C. Only J.D. wasn't joking—he actually poisons her. Veronica helps J.D. forge a fake suicide note, hoping to put the whole sordid event behind them. But J.D. is just warming up. He keeps murdering popular kids, staging his kills to look like suicides, while Veronica stands by and watches (and is sometimes tricked into helping). Eventually, she realizes that there might be something wrong with J.D. She decides to break up with him using the old "it's not me, it's the fact that you like to kill people" explanation, so J.D. tries to kill her (big surprise) and the entire school. Luckily, Veronica saves everyone except for J.D. who blows himself up with his own bomb. Veronica goes back to school, dedicated to being nicer and making the school clique-free.

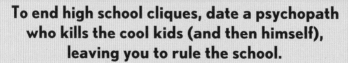

LIFE LESSON

**To end high school cliques, date a psychopath
who kills the cool kids (and then himself),
leaving you to rule the school.**

Which of the following does Veronica find the most attractive about J.D.?

a. When he brings an unloaded gun to school and pulls it on the football jocks as a joke.

b. When he claims gas station food keeps him sane.

c. When he compliments her talent for forging fake suicide notes.

d. When he takes her on a romantic date that involves murder.

Answer: All of the above. Psychopaths can be so hot.

Veronica (Winona Ryder) shares a smoke with her bloodthirsty, explosive-happy loverboy J.D. (Christian Slater). Ah, teen love.

SOUND BITE

VERONICA *[praying over Heather C.'s casket]*: Hi, I'm sorry. Technically, I did not kill Heather Chandler, but, hey, who am I trying to kid, right? I just want my high school to be a nice place. Amen ... Did that sound bitchy?

Say Anything... 1989

igh school senior Lloyd is an all-around nice guy, kick boxer, and low achiever. While everyone else is making post-graduation plans, his top priority is to date Diane, a gorgeous brainiac who his friends agree has "the body of a game-show hostess." Diane seems unattainable until after graduation day, when Lloyd finally mans-up and asks her out.

They start dating, even though Diane is leaving in the fall for a prestigious fellowship in England. Lloyd falls hopelessly in love, and right as he's saying "I love you" for the first time, Diane breaks up with him (to focus on her future). He's devastated. To get her back, he calls her. She won't take his call, so he calls her again. And again. After leaving her several unanswered messages, he shows up at her house, stands on her lawn, and blasts Peter Gabriel's "In Your Eyes" from a boombox that he holds over his head. Diane still needs a few days to think about it (and deal with her father getting arrested for swindling old people), but Lloyd's obsessive persistence pays off. She finally takes him back—and then takes him with her to England.

LIFE LESSON

If a girl breaks up with you, stalk her until she changes her mind, and try to get in on her next overseas trip.

Lloyd proves himself to be a perfect boyfriend because he's:

a. Patient. He teaches her how to drive her new stick-shift car and, even when she's ruining the car, rewards her with kisses.

b. Sensitive. His best friends are girls.

c. Strong. Holding a boombox above your head for an entire song is strenuous.

d. Flexible. He has zero scheduling conflicts that inhibit him from tagging along on Diane's trip to England.

Answer: All of the above. If you're going to have a boyfriend who has no future plans, he might as well be a babe like Lloyd.

Lloyd (John Cusack) trespasses onto his honey's front lawn, and blasts Peter Gabriel through the speakers on his boombox.

SOUND BITE

D.C. (Lloyd's friend): Look, why don't you just call Diane again?

LLOYD: I draw the line at seven unreturned phone calls.

Don't Tell Mom the Babysitter's Dead

1991 312272

High school graduate Sue Ellen is thrilled that her mother is going on vacation for the summer, until she finds out that her mom hired a crotchety, old babysitter to take care of her and her four younger siblings. Luckily, the babysitter soon dies in her sleep. So Sue Ellen and her siblings drop the dead body off at the morgue's doorstep, agree not to tell their mother, and hope to continue on with an awesome summer. Until they realize all the money their mother left them was in the sweater pocket of the dead babysitter. Whoops.

To earn some cash, Sue Ellen cons her way into a fashion executive job, where she lies to her coworkers daily to cover up her real age and lack of experience. Then she starts dating Bryan, a sweet guy whose sister happens to work with Sue Ellen, and lies to him about who she is, as well. The whole mess unravels when her mom comes home early to find Sue Ellen hosting a high scale fashion event in her backyard. But instead of getting in trouble, Sue Ellen gets a job offer, her mother's respect, and a rose from Bryan.

LIFE LESSON

To find happiness, simply cover up a death, defraud a company, and lie to everyone you know.

Sue Ellen (Christina Applegate) pawns off some of her workload to her coworker Cathy (Kimmy Robertson). It's hard to be a fake fashion executive.

Sue Ellen's Guide to Successfully Lying About Your Age

1. Forge a résumé.
2. Trick your coworkers into doing the work you don't actually know how to do.
3. Refer to your brothers and sisters as "my children."
4. Hide your ID at all costs.
5. Practice the heartfelt apologies you'll deliver when your cover is inevitably blown.

SOUND BITE

BRYAN: I'd respect your privacy if you weren't so secretive.

SUE ELLEN: Well, I'd tell you more if you didn't want to know so much.

Buffy the 1992 Vampire Slayer

B uffy, a ditzy Los Angeles high school cheerleader, must become a vampire slayer, according to Merrick, a mysterious guy in a trench coat who tracks Buffy down at the mall and claimes to be her "watcher." Buffy is not psyched. Learning to stake a heart from ten feet away is hardly at the top of her priority list. But suddenly she's haunted daily by vamps, so she gives in and begins to learn the art of slaying.

Soon, she starts killing vampires, usually in a cheerleading uniform or some other cute outfit. It's going well, and Buffy even saves the life of a local punk named Pike, who becomes her partner in slaying. But then the master vampire, Lothos, kills Merrick. Buffy is devastated and swears off the slayer gig, trying to resume her normal teen existence by going to the senior dance. Of course, Lothos and his army of vamps show up to wreak havoc, and Buffy realizes that she can't escape her destiny. So, in her poofy white prom dress, she stakes Lothos with a broken chair leg and then takes off on the back of Pike's motorcycle to go celebrate.

LIFE LESSON

If you're forced into a life of killing vampires, at least look hot while doing it.

BUFFY: Oh, wow. I ... I never hit anybody before.

MERRICK: Really? Well, you did it perfectly.

BUFFY: I didn't even break a nail.

In her cute cheerleading uniform, Buffy (Kristy Swanson) heads to the cemetery to stake a creepy vamp through the heart. Go team!

Which of the following is the most important element of Buffy's slayer training?

a. Boxing.

b. Gymnastics.

c. Staking.

d. Fashion accessorizing.

Answer: d. You'll never know when you need to save a cute boy's life.

Encino Man 1992

312272

At Encino High School, seniors Dave and Stoney rank lowest on the popularity totem pole. But Dave is determined to graduate high school a legend, so he starts building an in-ground swimming pool in his backyard (to impress his classmates) and sets his sights on taking the popular hottie, Robyn, to prom. Then, one day, while digging in Dave's backyard, Dave and Stoney uncover a frozen (but alive) caveman. After giving him a bath and dressing him, they enroll their prehistoric friend in school as a foreign exchange student named Link.

Link is barely verbal, mesmerized by fire, and eats frogs and dog food: This makes him instantly popular. His unpretentious ways are a hit with the ladies, and Robyn decides to go to prom with him. Dave is bummed, but eventually gives his blessing. Then, at the prom, Robyn's ex-boyfriend, Matt (who found out about Link's prehistoric pedigree), decides to expose Link for who he is, but no one seems to care. Matt and Dave get into a scuffle on stage and Matt punches Dave in the face. Then, Dave, Link, and Stoney lead the crowd in an impromptu (yet intricately choreographed) dance. Robyn, impressed with Dave's heroism and dance skills, finally gives him a chance.

LIFE LESSON

Grunt like a caveman to get the girl. Get punched in the face to keep her.

Stoney *[on Link's first day at school]*: Poor stone-ager, he spent a million years chillin' in a block of ice, now he's got to go to high school.

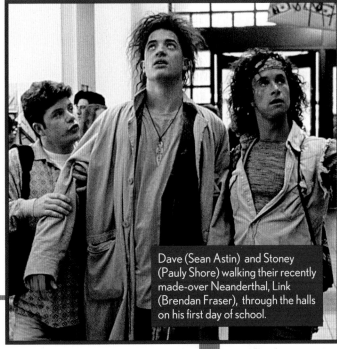

Dave (Sean Astin) and Stoney (Pauly Shore) walking their recently made-over Neanderthal, Link (Brendan Fraser), through the halls on his first day of school.

Which of the following items does Link put in his mouth during the course of the movie?

a. Prom flowers.

b. Bath beads.

c. Gutter water.

d. A tub of margarine.

e. A frog.

f. Dog food.

g. An entire bowl of salsa.

Answer: All of the above. Sexy!

Dazed and Confused 1993

Mitch and Sabrina are incoming freshmen at Lee High School in Austin, Texas, and they want what any new freshman wants: to be cool with the seniors. It's easy—all they have to do is suffer a little hazing. So Mitch and his friends get their butts paddled raw by the senior guys (with each senior's customized wooden paddle). Then, Sabrina, along with a pack of other freshman girls, is ordered to lie face down in the school's parking lot and flop on the ground like a strip of frying bacon, while being sprayed with hot-dog condiments.

It's pretty humiliating, but afterward the most popular seniors in school invite Mitch and Sabrina to drive around and party the rest of the night. Sabrina gets late-night pancakes with a senior boy who kisses her on her front lawn, while Mitch scores beer for the senior guys and spends a hot night on a picnic blanket with a pretty sophomore girl.

LIFE LESSON

Letting seniors haze the crap out of you is your ticket to being popular and finding love.

SIMONE *[senior girl, talking to freshman girls on the ground covered in hot-dog condiments]*: I did it when I was a freshman, and you'll do it when you're seniors. But you're doing great. Now fry like bacon, you little freshman piggies! Fry!

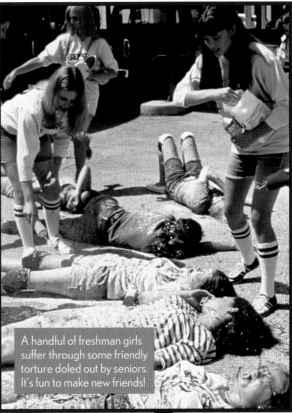

A handful of freshman girls suffer through some friendly torture doled out by seniors. It's fun to make new friends!

Mitch and Sabrina's Top Tips for Freshman Year

1. Drink away the sting of homemade wooden paddles with cheap beer.

2. Learn to enjoy being verbally harassed by idiots.

3. Always have an extra set of clothes on hand in case you are unwillingly doused in condiments. (If you don't, let seniors run you through a carwash.)

4. Make out with upperclassmen who you barely know.

5. Smile. It doesn't get any better than this!

Clueless  1995

Beautiful 15-year-old Cher is a ditzy girl who lives in a Beverly Hills mansion with unlimited spending money, a closet full of designer clothes, and a new car (despite not having her license). She considers breaking in a new pair of shoes a big accomplishment. When not shopping, Cher's favorite hobby is meddling in other people's lives for her own benefit. For instance, she tries to set up two lonely teachers, thinking that if they were less lonely, they'd give out less homework and better grades. Cher is super popular, but her smart, flannel-clad, socially conscious ex-stepbrother, Josh, hates everything she stands for.

One day, Josh accuses Cher of never doing anything that doesn't serve her own personal interest. She decides to prove him wrong, which in Cher's brain means taking a new transfer student under her wing, making her over, and inducting her into Cher's materialistic clique. That plan backfires, but Cher keeps trying and, in the end, she does become nicer to the kids at school. She also decides that she is in love with Josh. And even though they still have nothing in common, Josh confesses he's in love with her, too.

LIFE LESSON

A smart, sensitive guy will eventually fall for a ditzy, self-serving girl as long as she promises to be a little nicer to people—and is ridiculously hot.

Which of the following about Cher impresses Josh the most?

a. Her extensive knowledge of Mel Gibson movies.

b. Her ability to use big words without knowing their meanings.

c. Her failure to pass a driver's test.

d. The way a short dress looks really good on her.

Answer: d. Common interests and values aren't that important for a successful relationship.

Cher (Alicia Silverstone) asks Josh (Paul Rudd) to help her practice her driving skills while he reads Nietzsche by the pool.

SOUND BITE

CHER: Would you call me selfish?

DIONNE *(her best friend)*: No ... not to your face.

The Craft 1996

312272

Sarah can make water pipes burst and pencils twirl on their tips with just her mind. So, when she moves with her father and stepmother to Los Angeles and meets three mysterious high school classmates who study magic—Bonnie, Rochelle, and Nancy—the four become fast friends. They begin experimenting with their powers, starting with giggly magic games, like changing their hair colors and casting various minor spells on classmates.

But then Nancy decides to invoke a great spirit called Manon—and goes crazy. Nancy morphs into Sarah to hook up with (and then kill) the resident obnoxious high school jock. Bonnie and Rochelle are distracted by their own powers and don't seem to care, but Sarah vows to stop Nancy from doing more damage. The two have a teen-witch-girl showdown and Sarah, who's able to invoke Manon to do good because she has a purer heart, kicks Nancy into a mirror and wins the fight. In the end, Nancy loses her powers and gets locked away in a mental institute; Bonnie and Rochelle lose all of their powers; and Sarah's back to not really having any friends.

LIFE LESSON

Magic powers mixed with hormonal teenage girls can only lead to dead boys and catastrophic catfights in which everyone ends up pissed or crazy.

Bonnie (Neve Campbell), Rochelle (Rachel True), Nancy (Fairuza Balk), and Sarah (Robin Tunney) playing nice together before they get drunk on teen witch power.

Which is Sarah's favorite memory of the fun times she had with her girlfriends in LA?

a. The time Nancy drove recklessly through the city, ran a red light, and almost killed them all.

b. The time her friends made her believe that her dad and stepmom had died in a plane crash.

c. The time her friends tried to convince her to kill herself.

d. The time her friends made her have hallucinations that snakes, cockroaches, and rats were crawling all over her house.

Answer: All of the above. Girls just wanna have fun!

I Know What You Did Last Summer

1997 312272

After a wild night of partying on the beach, four high school grads—Helen, Barry, Ray, and Julie—encounter the ultimate buzz kill: They accidentally hit a stranger crossing the windy road with their car. Julie, the straight-laced good girl of the group, begs to report the accident, but the other three craft the most logical, fail-proof plan ever: Dump the dead body in the harbor and never speak of the night again. But right before rolling the body off the harbor deck, it springs to life. So what do they do? Push the live person into the water and go home.

One year later, Julie receives an ominous letter reading, "I know what you did last summer!" Turns out that the guy they hit—a crazy man in a fishing coat named Ben—is still alive and pissed about that night on the dock. To get revenge, Ben (who's not a stranger to homicide) murders Barry, Helen, and various other townspeople during the course of the summer, using a giant, silver fishing hook. Ray and Julie survive the summer, but can't manage to actually kill Ben (again), so they are forced to live in fear.

LIFE LESSON

If you're going to accidently run over a psychopath and dump his body in a harbor, make sure he is actually dead.

When do Helen, Barry, Ray, and Julie advocate for calling the police?

a. The moment you run someone over.

b. After you realize the person you hit isn't actually dead and your friends want to drown him in the harbor.

c. When that same person ends up surviving the harbor and starts mailing you threatening letters.

d. When that same person starts killing your friends.

Answer: None of the above. Who needs police?

Ray (Freddie Prinze Jr.), Julie (Jennifer Love Hewitt), Helen (Sarah Michelle Gellar), and Barry (Ryan Phillippe) realize they have just hit a stranger with their car. 911 anyone? Nah.

SOUND BITE

BARRY *[after Julie shows him the note from Ben]*: How do you know this is even related? You did a lot of things last summer.

JULIE: Yeah, well, only one murder comes to mind.

Can't Hardly Wait 1998

312272

At Huntington Hills High School, four graduating seniors each hate something about the last four years. Preston, the wide-eyed romantic, has been in love with Amanda ever since freshman year, but he never made a move and this jock, Mike, swooped her up. Preston's best friend, Denise, is a cynical outsider who can't stand the rest of her classmates. The high school nerd, William, is a punching bag for Amanda's jock boyfriend. And Kenny, the goofy poser, can't seem to get laid.

Fast forward to graduation night, where all four wind up at the same party with intentions of finally turning things around. Amanda—dumped by Mike—is single for the first time in four years, and Preston is bent on telling her how he feels. Denise wants to prove to herself that her fellow students might not be so bad. William plans to humiliate Mike with an elaborate revenge plan, and Kenny is determined to lose his virginity. And by the next morning, they all (pretty much) get what they want.

LIFE LESSON

No matter your high school social status, love, popularity, revenge, and sex are all yours on graduation night.

PRESTON: Amanda and I are connected. We have been, ever since the first day that she came to school.

DENISE: Oh, God. Here we go.

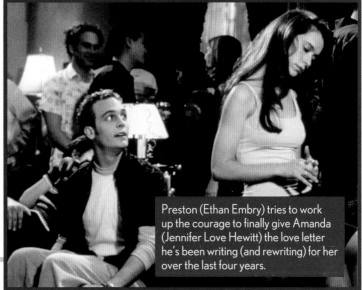

Preston (Ethan Embry) tries to work up the courage to finally give Amanda (Jennifer Love Hewitt) the love letter he's been writing (and rewriting) for her over the last four years.

Preston believes that he and Amanda are destined to be together because:

a. The first time he saw her, they were both eating strawberry Pop-Tarts.

b. Her boyfriend dumped her on the same night that Preston and Amanda are, for the first time, going to be at a party together.

c. On the night of the party, he hears the Barry Manilow song "Mandy" on the radio.

d. At the party, he drops the letter he wrote to her in the trash, but it miraculously winds up on the table in front of her a few minutes later.

Answer: All of the above. He clearly doesn't know the meaning of "coincidence."

Jawbreaker 1999

312272

On the morning of Liz's 17th birthday, her crew of popular friends—Courtney, Julie, and Marcie—break into her house, bind her limbs, and stuff her in the car trunk to treat her to a pancake breakfast before school. Courtney also shoves an enormous jawbreaker into Liz's mouth and covers it with duct tape, as a joke. It might have been funny—if Liz didn't choke to death.

Julie and Marcie are panicked, but Courtney simply calls the school and says Liz is home sick, then instructs the girls to put Liz's dead body back into her bed and make it look like the result of a kinky sex-romp gone wrong. When a nerdy girl named Fern comes to drop off Liz's homework assignments, she sees what's going on. Courtney buys her silence by bribing her with the promise of popularity. Then, to assure the cops believe the "deadly sex" story, Courtney lures a random guy to Liz's room, has sex with him (Liz's body is under the bed), and gives his name to the cops. Her plan works, until Julie, who's been against the cover-up all along, exposes Courtney on prom night as the real killer—just as she's being crowned prom queen. Courtney's adoring public starts screaming insults and throwing corsages at her. She runs out of the auditorium sobbing effusively in her perfect aqua-blue prom dress.

LIFE LESSON

It's an inconvenience when you accidentally kill your friend, but true devastation is losing your popularity.

According to Courtney, the worst part about Liz's death is that:

a. It's her fault.

b. It happens on Liz's birthday.

c. Liz's parents are out of town and have to return to the horror of their daughter dead in her bed.

d. The trauma breaks up their crew and saddens the whole school.

Answer: Who cares that Liz is dead? Courtney's prom was totally ruined!

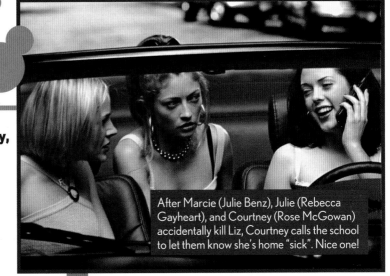

After Marcie (Julie Benz), Julie (Rebecca Gayheart), and Courtney (Rose McGowan) accidentally kill Liz, Courtney calls the school to let them know she's home "sick". Nice one!

SOUND BITE

COURTNEY *[talking to the girls the morning of the murder]*:
OK, reality check. Liz is in the trunk of this car. And she's dead. That is a sad, f—ked up thing, but you're going to walk into that school and strut your s—t down the hall-way like everything is peachy f—king keen.

American Pie 1999

312272

Jim and his friends are sick of being virgins, so they make a pact to lose their V-cards by graduation. Jim, the least experienced of the group, has horrible sexual luck. His mom catches him masturbating with a sock and his father walks in on him "experimenting" with an apple pie. He's obsessed with a foreign exchange student named Nadia, and when he finally has a chance to hook up with her, he broadcasts it live on the internet for his friends to see. But it's not exactly his shining sexual moment, since he gets a little *too* excited *too* quickly. And then, the video accidentally gets sent around to the entire school. Jim's a laughing stock, and Nadia gets sent home to Czechoslovakia.

Humiliated and dateless, Jim asks Michelle, a geeky marching band member, to prom because he thinks she might be the only girl in school who hasn't seen his awkward internet debut. But Michelle actually has seen it and thinks Jim's desperation is a turn-on. At the prom after-party, they have wild sex and Jim wakes up alone, clutching an inflatable dinosaur. Sure, Michelle used him, but he doesn't care—he's just happy to have lost his virginity.

LIFE LESSON

Masturbating with an apple pie and broadcasting your sexual failures online will get you laid on prom night.

JIM *[waking up alone the morning after prom night]*: She's gone. Oh my God, she used me. I was used. I was used! Cool!

Jim (Jason Biggs) is excited to hook up with Nadia (Shannon Elizabeth). A little bit *too* excited.

Jim's Guide to Becoming a Desirable Prom Date

1. Avoid any contact with real girls before senior year.

2. Warm up for prom with things like socks and attractive-looking pastries.

3. If, by some chance, you do end up with a real girl pre-prom night, make sure the event is a spectacular failure.

4. Remember said failure has more potency if your entire school watches it online.

5. Sit back as the sexually adventurous band geek attacks you.

Drive Me Crazy 1999

Nicole and Chase are next-door neighbors and used to be best friends in elementary school, but as high school seniors, they barely speak. Ultra-popular Nicole spends all of her time planning the school's 100-year anniversary dance, and trying to get Brad, a hot basketball player, to ask her to be his date. Chase, the nonconformist, prefers planning pranks with his friends and hanging out with his edgy, activist girlfriend Dulcie. Then, in the same week, Brad falls in love with a rival school's cheerleader, leaving Nicole dateless for the dance and Dulcie dumps Chase, claiming he's not rebellious enough.

To save themselves from public disgrace, Nicole proposes she and Chase pretend to start dating each other. Chase gets a "popular guy" makeover and the two begin appearing together at parties and school basketball games. But when Dulcie and Brad try to reenter the picture, the fake couple realizes they have real feelings for each other, and decide to become a real (like really real) couple. Then, Chase's dad and Nicole's mom announce that they have fallen in love (weird, considering they never mentioned that they were dating) and that they're all moving in together. Nicole and Chase run off to celebrate their impending step-sibling-hood by getting busy in the tree house.

LIFE LESSON

**To find true love, fake it till you make it.
Then, move in together as siblings.**

Nicole and Chase's Five-Step Guide to Fake Dating

1. Go to parties together.

2. Sing along to songs on the radio together.

3. Hold hands while walking into social events.

4. Kiss to make each other's exes uncomfortable.

5. Realize that doing the above means you are actually dating.

Nicole (Melissa Joan Hart) and Chase (Adrian Grenier) out on the town, "pretending" to be a couple.

SOUND BITE

MRS. MARIS *(Nicole's mom)*: We're moving in together.

NICOLE: What?

MR. HAMMOND *(Chase's dad)*: Maybe we should think about this.

NICOLE: Okay, you think about it here and we'll think about it in the tree house.

Never Been Kissed

1999

312272

Josie is a 25-year-old reporter at the *Chicago Sun-Times* who spends her free time sewing pillows and waiting for her first great kiss. She's just been assigned her first feature story: an undercover exposé on the secret life of high schoolers. She's excited—until she remembers that her high school nickname was "Josie Gross-y" and the most popular guy in school threw eggs at her on prom night.

Josie takes the assignment anyway. She enrolls as a student and even manages to become popular. She also discovers the joys of flirting with her young, hockey-playing English teacher, Sam. They flirt while discussing Shakespeare, painting the school play backdrop, and even slow dancing together at the prom. Josie's newspaper editor sees what's up and changes the story's focus, against Josie's will, to lecherous teacher-student relationships. But at the prom, Sam finds out about Josie's real age and her undercover story on him. He's furious that she betrayed him (though never apologizes for having flirted with a student). At the last minute, Josie changes her news story into an essay about her undercover experience. In it, she confesses her true feelings for Sam, and asks him to meet her on the baseball mound before a big game for her first great kiss. Sam shows up and everyone cheers.

LIFE LESSON

Inappropriate teacher-student relationships are totally acceptable as long as the student is a desperate, undercover reporter.

SAM: All I can tell you is that when you're my age, guys will be lined up around the corner for you.

JOSIE: You have to say that because you're my teacher.

SAM: Actually, I shouldn't say that because I'm your teacher.

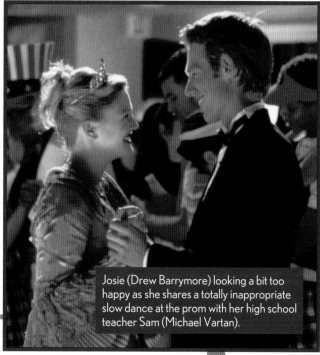

Josie (Drew Barrymore) looking a bit too happy as she shares a totally inappropriate slow dance at the prom with her high school teacher Sam (Michael Vartan).

Sam should probably worry about his job security when he:

a. Stares longingly at Josie as she talks about Shakespeare.

b. Takes a romantic ferris wheel ride alone with Josie.

c. Runs into Josie and other students out at a nightclub.

d. Makes out with a former "student" on top of a baseball mound.

Answer: Oh, come on. Who's going to fire such a cute guy?

Varsity Blues

1999

312212

Jonathan "Mox" Moxon is a second-string quarterback on his high school football team in West Canaan, Texas. He's basically a bench warmer, which is fine with Mox because he doesn't have to deal much with the team's lunatic coach, Bud Kilmer. Then the star quarterback, Lance, blows out his knee—and Mox becomes the starting QB.

Signing autographs and having girls throw themselves at him is fun until Mox realizes that being star QB means obeying Kilmer, who bullies players to compete even when they have multiple concussions and torn ligaments, and injects them with harmful drugs to keep them on the field. As the season goes on, Mox also finds out that Kilmer is a racist, setting up college agent visits only for the white players. None of the players report any of the abuse, but Mox finally stands up to Kilmer during the championship game halftime, and demands that the coach step down. Kilmer flies into a psychotic rage and tries to strangle Mox in the locker room. Luckily, Mox's teammates are able to pick the coach off before he kills Mox, and the team goes on to win the game without a coach.

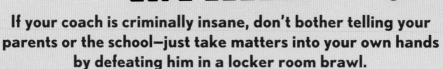

LIFE LESSON

If your coach is criminally insane, don't bother telling your parents or the school—just take matters into your own hands by defeating him in a locker room brawl.

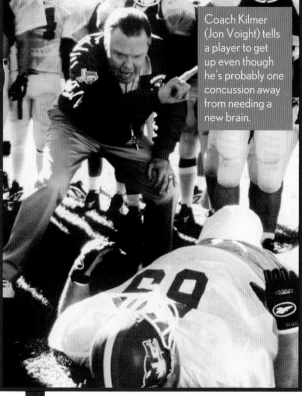

Coach Kilmer (Jon Voight) tells a player to get up even though he's probably one concussion away from needing a new brain.

At the end of the movie:

a. Coach Kilmer is fired for abusing his players.

b. Coach Kilmer is tried in court for racial discrimination.

c. Coach Kilmer is arrested for assaulting a high school student.

d. The statue of Coach Kilmer is taken down.

Answer: None of the above. Kilmer simply retires and his statue is apparently too heavy to move.

SOUND BITE

COACH KILMER *[in a "pep talk" to his players]*: Never show weakness. The only pain that matters is the pain you inflict.

She's All That 1999

312272

Zack, student body president and the school's soccer star, is used to being top dog at Harrison High School (there's even a framed picture of him in the hallway). So when his girlfriend, prom queen front-runner Taylor, dumps him for a reality TV star she met on spring break, Zack is humiliated.

Zack attempts reputation damage control by bragging to his friends that Taylor is nothing special. He even bets his friend Dean that he can turn any girl into prom queen. She just needs him as a boyfriend, and a good makeover. Dean accepts the bet and picks Laney—a militant social activist and self-professed "art dork" who works at a falafel hut. Zack melts Laney's skeptical heart by pretending to be interested in interpretative performance art and protecting her geeky younger brother from high school bullies. Then Zack's sister gives Laney a hot makeover. Suddenly, Zack starts to actually like her. But Dean tells her about the bet, so Laney dumps Zack and goes to the prom with Dean (and loses prom queen). Later that night, Zack shows up at her house, apologizes for being a moron, and they slow dance in Laney's backyard.

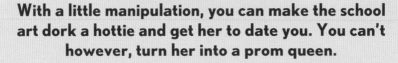

LIFE LESSON

With a little manipulation, you can make the school art dork a hottie and get her to date you. You can't however, turn her into a prom queen.

What lies does Zach tell Laney?

a. That he likes performance art.

b. That he likes standing up for wimpy students.

c. That he likes going to parties with her.

d. That he has no ulterior motive.

Answer: These weren't lies, just dating techniques.

Zack (Freddie Prinze Jr.) shows up at Laney's job at the falafel hut to try and convince Laney (Rachael Leigh Cook) to date him. As part of a bet. Nice guy.

10 Things I Hate About You

1999

312272

Cameron, a new student at Padua High, is in love with sophomore hottie Bianca. But Bianca's dad has a rule: She can't start dating until her older sister, Kat, does. And Kat—an anti-social, ultra-feminist, aspiring musician into riot grrrl music—hasn't a romantic prospect in sight. So, Cameron devises a plan. He tricks Joey, a conceited rich kid who is also interested in Bianca, to pay the high school bad boy, Patrick, to take Kat out. Cameron convinces Joey that this will give him a chance with Bianca.

Kat and Patrick start dating, and Patrick realizes that he likes Kat and her abrasive, no BS persona. Meanwhile, Cameron wins Bianca's heart. The happy couples go to the prom, but then Kat finds about about the scheme and dumps Patrick. Later that week, Kat reads a poem in front of her English class (Patrick included) confessing the 10 things she hates about a certain unnamed guy, including the fact that she doesn't hate him at all. Patrick realizes the poem is about him, so he buys Kat a guitar with the money Joey gave him, and they get back together.

LIFE LESSON
Money can buy you love. And it's even better if it's someone else's money.

Patrick's Guide to Wooing a Feisty Woman

1. Never be afraid, despite her reputation for kicking male students in the balls.

2. Brush up on your witty remarks; otherwise her biting sarcasm will destroy you.

3. If she's mad at you, humiliate yourself by serenading her with "Can't Take My Eyes Off of You" with the marching band as your backup.

4. Take her on a paint-ball date to work out some of her aggression.

5. When in doubt, buy her stuff. Even angry girls like presents.

Kat (Julia Stiles) overhears Joey (Andrew Keegan) and Patrick (Heath Ledger) talking about how Patrick was paid to take her out. She's not happy.

SOUND BITE

KAT: You can't just buy me a guitar every time you screw up, you know?

PATRICK: Yeah, I know. But then, you know, there's always drums, and bass, and maybe even one day a tambourine.

Bring It On 2000

312272

Perky, blonde Torrance is the new captain of her San Diego cheer squad, the Toros—the reigning national champion squad for five years, known for its highly original cheers. Then Missy, a gymnast from urban LA, joins the squad. At her first practice, Missy instantly recognizes the cheers: They belong to a little-known, black LA cheer squad named the Clovers. It seems that the previous Toros captain had been stealing cheers.

Torrance doesn't know what to do. The hot-headed captain of the Clovers, Isis, is out for blood and Torrance doesn't want to be a cheer-stealer anyway. But the Toros have no original cheers. Or ideas. So Torrance pays an obnoxious choreographer named Sparky to teach her squad a new routine to perform at the regional competition. The team is humiliated when they find out Sparky has sold the exact same routine to five other California squads. With no other hope, the Toros are forced to actually come up with their own cheers for the national competition. In less than three weeks, they create a routine that gets them second place at Nationals. The Clovers, who have been training honestly for the event for years, do snag first—but just by a hair.

LIFE LESSON

Even if you get caught stealing routines, and have no choreographic experience, you can still take second place at a national cheer competition.

How do the Toros choreograph their sucsuccessful Nationals routine?

a. By leaving themselves plenty of practice time.

b. By relying on their past experiences.

c. By hiring a professional cheer coach.

d. By watching old musicals, and cramming swing dance, interpretative dance, and miming lessons into three weeks and then throwing something together.

Answer: d. With enough cheer spirit, you can apparently pull off anything.

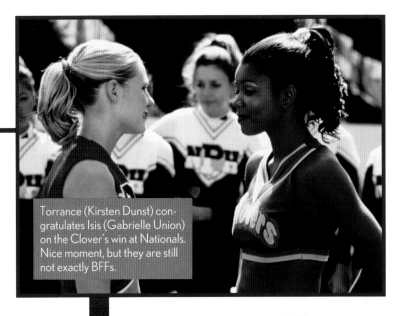

Torrance (Kirsten Dunst) congratulates Isis (Gabrielle Union) on the Clover's win at Nationals. Nice moment, but they are still not exactly BFFs.

Whatever It Takes *2000*

312272

Ryan and Maggie are best friends and next-door neighbors who spend a lot of time talking about Maggie's lack of dating prospects and Ryan's obsession with Ashley, the school's queen bee. Then Ashley's popular cousin Chris offers to help Ryan score a date with Ashley—if Ryan will help him get Maggie. (Maggie's the only girl in school who's resistant to Chris' cocky charm.) Ryan agrees and the manipulation-fest begins.

Ashley digs jerks, so Chris helps Ryan insult her. Maggie likes sensitive intellectuals, so Ryan helps Chris pretend that he loves volunteering with old people. The boys' BS is working—until Ryan realizes he loves Maggie. (It doesn't help that Ashley turns out to be rude, bratty, and prone to rashes.) Also, Ryan finds out that Chris is only after sex, so he feels really bad about the whole scheme. He confesses everything to Maggie, but she's furious about what he's done, and still goes to prom with Chris. But when Chris gets sleazy at the hotel prom after-party, Maggie leaves him blindfolded and publically tied to a bed in his underwear. Later that night, when Ryan sees that Maggie's home, he jumps onto her balcony and offers a two-minute apology. She forgives him, and they make out.

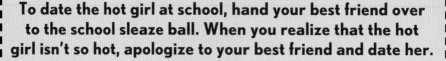

LIFE LESSON

To date the hot girl at school, hand your best friend over to the school sleaze ball. When you realize that the hot girl isn't so hot, apologize to your best friend and date her.

CHRIS *[jumping across from his bedroom balcony to Maggie's to apologize]*: Maggie, I need to talk to you.

MAGGIE: What, lying and cheating weren't enough? Now you're breaking and entering?

Maggie (Marla Sokoloff) forgiving Ryan (Shane West) even after he pawned her off on the school's biggest creep.

Ryan questions his interest in super hot Ashley when she:

a. Pukes on him during a carnival ride and acts like it's cute.

b. Thoughtlessly refers to him as Brian, despite his multiple reminders that his name is Ryan.

c. Demands that he dump his geeky friends in order to date her.

d. Touches him with her feet, which are covered in a disgusting rash.

Answer: All of the above. Ryan's a little slow on the uptake.

Save the Last Dance 2001

Sara used to be a ballerina with dreams of attending Juilliard, a prestigious performing arts school. But on the day of her audition, Sara's mother dies in a car wreck (rushing to meet Sara there). Sara guiltily gives up ballet and moves to the South Side of Chicago to live with her estranged jazz musician father.

Sara struggles as a white girl in a predominately black crowd, but a few kids at her school, including a cute overachiever named Derek, step in and help update her look and dancing style to fit in at the hip-hop club. While Sara and Derek have flirty dance-offs, she starts showing off her old ballet moves, and Derek convinces her to re-audition for Julliard. But right before the big audition, the two have a big fight about the hardships of being an interracial couple, which makes Sara even more stressed than she already is. When she starts to perform, she screws up majorly. Derek's watching from the back and, when he sees her start to choke, he runs up on stage to give her a pep talk—in the middle of her audition. Despite the interruption, the judges allow Sara to finish her now flawless hip-hop inspired ballet number and then practically accept her on the spot.

LIFE LESSON

To get into a highly competitive dance academy, get overly emotional before your audition, dance poorly, and then have your boyfriend interrupt in the most unprofessional way imaginable.

If this had been a real audition, the Julliard judges would have:

a. Said, "Next!" after Sara loses her balance and almost falls over.

b. Told Derek to get his butt off the stage.

c. Laughed when Sara asks for a second chance.

d. Told Sara they'll contact her to let her know how she does, rather than telling her the results on the spot.

Answer: None of the above. Getting into a top tier dance academy is cake!

Derek (Sean Patrick Thomas) teaching Sara (Julia Stiles) to dance hip-hop before he almost ruins her Juilliard audition.

Sugar & Spice 2001

At Lincoln High School, disgruntled B-squad cheerleader Lisa can't stand the school's golden couple: Diane (the A-squad cheer captain) and Jack (the star quarterback), which she refers to as "Barbie and Ken, but without the pink, remote control Corvette." She thinks they're too perfect for their own good, and also thinks that Diane, who breaks national cheerleading rules, should be taking orders from her.

So when Jack gets Diane pregnant, Lisa's feeling pretty smug. The couple's parents kick them out, and they're suddenly broke and struggling. To get some money, Diane and her squad decide to rob the bank branch where she works part-time, located in the local grocery store. The girls study robbery techniques from gangster movies, get tips from actual criminals, and even make a "craft project" out of fixing up some junky old guns to pull off their heist. But Lisa is in the grocery store during the robbery and recognizes the masked girls after they use a cheer stunt to wipe out the surveillance cameras. Now, she can negotiate with Diane for what she really wants: A-squad captain status. She offers Diane a deal: She'll be the girls' alibi under the condition that she takes Diane's place as A-squad captain when Diane gets too pregnant to cheer. Diane agrees and Lisa proudly snatches the coveted title of head cheerleader.

LIFE LESSON

If you can't naturally get the spot you want on your high school sports team, blackmail your pregnant, bank-robbing classmate.

We should root for Lisa to become A-squad captain because:

a. She has a horrible attitude and gives the stink-eye to practically everyone.

b. She had plastic surgery over the summer to help her get a spot on the A-squad.

c. She laughs when Diane accidentally kicks Jack in the head during a cheer stunt.

d. She's a con artist who resorts to bribery to get what she wants.

Answer: All of the above. Aren't the best leaders shallow, cruel, and manipulative?

Lisa (Marla Sokoloff) happy to finally be A-squad captain. Even if she got there by blackmail.

SOUND BITE

DIANE: It was silly to think we could learn to rob a bank from watching movies. Sex—you can learn from movies. But robberies? There's no way.

The Hot Chick 2002

312272

J essica is the hottest and meanest cheerleader in high school who flirts to get whatever she wants, and steals things when flirting fails. But one day, she shoplifts an ancient pair of earrings that have a magic spell on them: If they get split up between two people, those people switch bodies with each other. She promptly loses one, which gets picked up by Clive, a bumbling criminal. The next morning—poof! Jessica wakes up in Clive's hairy man-body.

Desperate to get her body back, "Jessica" (in Clive's body) and her friends talk to two fellow students Jessica's always tormented—a nerdy brainiac and a scary Wiccan girl—figuring her body-switching strife must be one of their revenge plans. They're not behind it, but they decide to help her after seeing that the pretty, popular girl is finally realizing there's more to life than outer beauty. On prom night, Jessica's friends find "Clive" dancing in a strip club (in Jessica's body) and "Jessica" (in Clive's body) steals the other earring back. Finally, Jessica has her hot body back. But her short-lived experience in Clive's body has changed her from a shallow jerk into a nicer, more thoughtful person.

LIFE LESSON
Stealing can be a deeply transformative experience, especially if it leads to body-swapping with a criminal.

The hardest part about being "Clive" is that Jessica has to:

a. Steal her dad's clothes.

b. Vigilantly trim her ear, nose, and chin hairs.

c. Constantly spray herself with deodorant to mask the "dude" smell.

d. Pay for her own coffee, because flirting with the coffee guy as "Clive" only results in being choked.

Answer: d. Male body maintenance is nothing compared to losing free drink privileges.

"Jessica" (Rob Schneider) asks her friend April (Anna Faris) to remove some unwanted facial hair.

SOUND BITE

APRIL (Jessica's friend): So... do you really have a penis?

JESSICA (as Clive): April!

APRIL: Can I see it?

JESSICA: What is the matter with you? I don't think you get the gravity of the situation here.

APRIL: You're right, you're right. I'm sorry. I'm sorry. Can I see it?

Love Don't Cost a Thing 2003

312272

Alvin is a smart, but dorky, high school senior who only gets invited to parties to clean the pool (his part-time job). But he's also an automotive expert, so when his dream girl, hot cheerleader Paris, accidentally wrecks her mother's Escalade, Alvin promises to fix it—if Paris pretends to date him. Paris reluctantly agrees to do it for 2 ½ weeks. During that time, Alvin gets a pimped-out makeover, develops a "popular guy" swagger, and takes on a new name (Al). Even Paris herself starts to fall for the stud she's created.

At the end of the 2 ½ weeks, Paris tries to suggest that they date for real, but Al has become so self-obsessed that he doesn't hear her. He sticks to the original plan, which involves a public breakup, and he humiliates Paris in the process. Then, he hooks up with her friend, ditches his old crowd, and abandons his studies. Fed up with his whole act, Paris tells everyone the truth about their date-for-hire plan. In a heartbeat, "Al" is back to "Alvin." After some sulking, he puts his old life back in order, and then makes a moving speech during a high school basketball game about the importance of individuality. Impressed by the speech, Paris forgives him and they get together for real.

LIFE LESSON

You can win the heart of a hot cheerleader by bribing her to date you, dissing her in front of the whole school, and then impressing her with a fancy speech.

ALVIN: Popularity is so much better than being a social leper.

Al (Nick Cannon), after breaking up with Paris, flirts with her friend Yvonne (Nichole Galicia).

Al's Guide to Becoming the Hottest Guy in School

1. Bribe the most popular girl in school to hang out with you for 2 ½ weeks.

2. Let her wax your unibrow.

3. Watch her tame your unruly 'fro, while you admire yourself in the mirror.

4. Have her take you shopping and replace your nerdy wardrobe with Sean John designer duds.

5. Forget that she's the only reason you're popular and arrogantly dismiss her in the hallways as your friends laugh.

Mean Girls 2004

312272

After growing up in Africa, 16-year-old Cady enters a public school in the US for the first time in her life. She becomes friends with two different cliques: the social misfits (Janis and Damien) and The Plastics, the exclusive, popular group led by Regina, the most idolized and feared girl in school.

Cady is intrigued by The Plastics at first, but she quickly becomes a target for Regina's manipulative games. To retaliate, Cady—egged on by Janis and Damien—starts scheming ways Cady can bring down The Plastics from the inside. Pretending to be Regina's friend, Cady gives Regina "weight loss" diet bars, which really have tons of calories, turns Regina's clique against her, and tells Regina's boyfriend that Regina is cheating (because Cady wants him for herself). Soon, Cady is the new top bitch of the school. Regina starts to strike back, and it becomes an all-out war. Then, when they are fighting in the middle of the street, a bus accidently hits Regina and half of the school blames Cady for the accident. That's when Cady realizes she's lost all of her friends and that everyone hates her. So, she apologizes to every-one at the Spring Fling dance, which sets everything right again.

LIFE LESSON

The best way to take the popular girl down: Be more abusive than she is. Then apologize to the whole school and all will be well.

How does Cady's upbringing in Africa prepare her for high school in the US?

a. The schools in Africa were top-notch.

b. Living in another country made her more open-minded.

c. Traveling taught her how to be independent.

d. Observing the monkeys, jaguars, and lions in the wild outback taught her how to fight for a prime spot on the high school food chain.

Answer: d. It's all about survival of the fittest when it comes to high school.

Cady (Lindsay Lohan) befriends The Plastics—Karen (Amanda Seyfried), Regina (Rachel McAdams), and Gretchen (Lacey Chabert)—before ruthlessly tearing them down.

The Girl Next Door 2004

312272

Matthew is a graduating senior and believes the ultimate high school experience involves partying, ditching class, getting wasted, and losing one's V-card. But he hasn't done any of that stuff. He's too busy practicing the speech that he hopes will win him the scholarship he needs to be able to afford Georgetown, where he was accepted for the fall.

Then a hot blonde girl, Danielle, who likes to undress in front of her open window, moves in next door. One look at her red thong makes Matt realize that she is going to change his life. In no time, Danielle has Matt streaking naked through the neighborhood, ditching class, and breaking into the school principal's backyard pool. Matt thinks he is in love with his new adrenaline junkie girlfriend until his friend breaks the news: Danielle is actually an ex-porn star. He tries to break it off, but realizes that Danielle and her crazy ways are good for him. (Plus, she is really hot.) In the end, he doesn't win the scholarship, but he does have sex in the back of a limo on prom night. He also gets Danielle's porn star friends to help him make a professional sex-ed video aimed at real teenagers. He ends up selling the video to high schools everywhere, making millions, and being able to afford Georgetown on his own.

LIFE LESSON

To pay for your college education, blow off school and date an ex-porn star with a passion for law-breaking —a business opportunity is bound to come out of it.

When Danielle's sleazy ex-boyfriend, Kelly (a porn producer), comes looking for her, which of the following happens to Matthew:

a. Kelly beats him up and tells him to leave Danielle alone.

b. Kelly secretly doses Matthew with ecstasy right before his scholarship speech.

c. Kelly forces Matthew to break into another porn producer's house and then calls the cops, almost getting Matthew arrested.

d. Kelly drains the fundraising bank account Matthew has for a school charity project.

Answer: All of the above. See? Dating Danielle is really exciting.

Danielle (Elisha Cuthbert) about to get undressed before an open window. Matthew watches and realizes he is in love.

SOUND BITE

DANIELLE: So, what's the craziest thing you've done lately?

MATTHEW: Oh, I mean, it's ... it's hard to tell, you know, because we've ... I've just done so much nuts stuff. I mean it's just off the hook, off the walls. I mean ...

DANIELLE: You haven't done anything, have you?

MATTHEW: No.

John Tucker Must Die 2006

J ohn Tucker is the captain of the basketball team at Forest Hills High School and a really good liar. He's dating three different girls at the same time: Beth, the vegan activist; Carrie, the future news reporter; and Heather, the head cheerleader. Each girl thinks she is John's only girlfriend. He almost gets away with it, until all three girls, plus Kate (a new girl in school who's witnessed John's triple-timing), coincidentally wind up in the same gym class one day.

Kate, who hates jerks (her mom always dates them), encourages the girls to get even. The four devise a plan to make over Kate to be John's fantasy girl and then mercilessly break his heart. Overnight, Kate becomes a confident cheerleader who plays hard to get. She and John start dating and the meaner she is to him, the more he starts to fall for her, enamored by the challenge. But all of the lying and manipulation makes Kate feel like a jerk. At John's giant birthday bash, she comes clean and John admits he's heartbroken. Seeing how it feels to get hurt, John vows to be more honest, which means he continues to date a lot of girls at once, but now he makes sure to tell them about each other.

LIFE LESSON

If you're a cheating womanizer with a broken heart, be honest about it, and you'll still find multiple girls willing to date you (at the same time).

John's Guide to Successful Womanizing

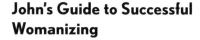

John Tucker (Jesse Metcalfe) with his exes, after he's sworn off his old ways. They don't look convinced.

1. Only date girls from different cliques to reduce the likelihood of them ever speaking. Hope they don't all end up in the same gym class.

2. Tell each of your ladies that the reason you need to keep your relationship a secret is because your dad forbids you from dating during basketball season.

3. Use pet names like "baby" and "sweetheart" to minimize name mix-ups.

4. Dump girls before they have a chance to find out you're cheating.

5. If anyone ever does find out, don't stress. Simply move on to the next girl.

SOUND BITE

JOHN *[talking to his two girlfriends after his change of heart]*: Now, we need to go into this with our eyes open, complete honesty. Jennifer, this is Jill ... my other girlfriend. I think we can make this work!

High School Musical 2006

312272

Troy is a basketball jock spending Christmas vacation with his family at a mountain resort. One night, he's pulled begrudgingly on stage to sing karaoke. Lucky for him, the random girl picked to be his duet partner is a cute girl named Gabriella, and they both have pitch-perfect pop-star voices and know how to professionally harmonize together without any experience or practice. Romance sparks, but when the evening is over, they part ways assuming they'll never see each other again.

When winter break ends, Troy finds out that Gabriella is a new student at his high school. Lucky again! They reunite and after remembering their shining moment while singing, they decide to audition for the high school musical together. But she's a brainiac and he's a jock and their friends think the two should stick to what they know. Then, the drama stars get threatened by the duo and try to sabotage them by changing the time of the auditions to conflict with the academic decathlon and the big basketball game. But, despite all of this, Gabriella and Troy still manage to make it to the auditions and win the lead roles in the play.

LIFE LESSON

With no vocal training or experience, a basketball jock and a bookish nerd can score the lead roles in a high school musical.

To prepare for their big audition, Troy and Gabriella:

a. Practice scales and other vocal exercises.

b. Sip hot water with lemon to soothe their throats.

c. Spend hours memorizing the lyrics for their audition songs.

d. Do nothing. They just decide at the last minute to run on stage and audition.

Answer: d. Professional-quality singing requires zero practice and effort when you're young and singing with your crush.

Troy (Zac Efron) and Gabriella (Vanessa Hudgens) singing karaoke together for the first time, unknowingly prepping for stardom.

SOUND BITE

GABRIELLA *[after Troy compliments her voice]*: Well, you sound like you've done a lot of singing, too.

TROY: Yeah, my shower-head is very impressed.

She's the Man 2006

Soccer player Viola wants to try out for the boys' team at her high school when the girls' team gets cancelled, but the school won't allow it. So she crafts a revenge plan: She's going to disguise herself as her twin brother, Sebastian (who is ditching the first two weeks of school to go to London with his band), show up at his boarding school, and try out for his soccer team (her school's rival team). She slaps on a boy's wig, tapes her boobs down, and learns how to walk, talk, and "think" like a guy.

Everyone buys the act, including her hot roommate, Duke. "Sebastian" and Duke become friends and Duke helps "Sebastian" train to make the soccer team. Meanwhile, Viola is starting to like (like, *like*) Duke and even flirts with him when she is in her regular girl form. Poor Duke doesn't make the connection. Then "Sebastian" convinces Duke to ask Viola (herself) out on a date. No one is any wiser until the real Sebastian comes home early from Europe, and blows her cover in the middle of the season's first soccer game. Everyone is upset about Viola's lies, but the coach lets her play in the game, which she helps win. And then, she scores Duke.

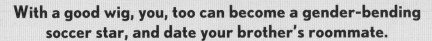

LIFE LESSON

With a good wig, you, too can become a gender-bending soccer star, and date your brother's roommate.

PAUL *[Viola's friend, coaching her on how to act like a guy]:* Just remember, inside every girl, there's a boy. That came out wrong but you know what I mean.

Paul (Jonathan Sadowski) coaching Viola (Amanda Bynes) as she gets ready for her first day of school as a dude.

Viola's cover should have been blown when:

a. Duke discovered a box of tampons in "Sebastian's" bag.

b. "Sebastian" refused to take "his" shirt off during soccer practice.

c. "Sebastian" started talking to Duke about subjects like relationships and heartbreak.

d. "Sebastian" refused to shower in the communal guys shower.

Answer: Wait—shouldn't someone have realized that Viola never showed up to her own school? A teacher? A parent? Anyone?

Twilight 2008

312272

Bella, the new girl in town, meets Edward, resident high school vampire. Edward is kind of a jerk, but excuses his behavior with the fact that he has uncontrollable desires to suck her blood. Enamored by Edward's glittery, ice-cold skin (and perhaps also his perfectly styled, gravity-defying hair), Bella sees beyond Edward's murderous tendencies, and decides to date him.

Things are great for a few days, but then evil rogue vampires show up and one of them tries to kill Bella. She gets bitten, which if left untreated would turn her into a vamp, but Edward shows up in time to suck the vamp-tainted blood out of her system. Of course, Edward's own bloodthirst almost kills her in the process, but he manages to stop himself from gorging and saves her life. Bella still ends up in the hospital with multiple injuries and no real promise that this type of thing won't keep happening, but she chooses to stay with Edward, because she's, like, really in love.

LIFE LESSON

**It's OK to date a dead, murderous vampire
so long as he's hot and has great hair.**

What injuries does Bella rack up throughout the movie?

a. A broken leg.

b. Broken ribs.

c. A cracked skull.

d. A vampire bite on her hand.

Answer: All of the above. Isn't love amazing?!

Edward (Robert Pattinson) tells Bella (Kristen Stewart) how he wants to both kill her and date her at the same time. Hot.

Youth in Revolt 2009

Dark and depressed Nick lives in Oakland, California, but is being forced to hide out in a trailer park in Clearlake, California, for a week with his mother and her con-artist boyfriend. It sucks, but then he meets a girl, Sheeni, and the two fall in love. When Nick has to return to Oakland, they make a plan: Sheeni will get Nick's unemployed dad a job near Clearlake, and Nick will get his mother so angry that she'll send him to go live with his dad.

Nick, who's a little unhinged, conjures up an imaginary alter ego named Francois Dillinger to do his dirty work. "Francois" causes an accident that sets fire to his mom's car, trailer, and a local storefront. The plan works—Nick gets sent to live with his dad, who now lives near Sheeni. But then, Sheeni's parents ship her off to boarding school. So "Francois" gets Sheeni expelled from school. But by the time she gets home, the cops are after Nick for the storefront fire. So, he tries, unsuccessfully, to stage his own suicide by stealing his father's car and sending it flying off a cliff (without him). The cops finally catch up with him. As Nick is dragged away, Sheeni reminds him that he's a minor and will be out in three months. And that she'll be waiting.

LIFE LESSON

Nothing's hotter than dating a 16-year-old guy with a split personality willing to commit crimes to be with you. (Downside: You have to wait for him while he's in juvee.)

NICK: Well, I'm headed for a stint in juvenile detention but I can at least be comforted by the fact that I'm not going in a virgin.

Nick and his imaginary alter ego "Francois" (both played by Michael Cera) watch as the car accident they caused creates a giant fire. Nick looks a bit disturbed, but Francois is really just warming up.

What is the most disturbing thing Nick does during his quest to be with Sheeni?

a. He flushes his mother's jewelry down the toilet and cuts all of her bras in half.

b. He unhinges his mother's car and trailer so that they cause a disastrous traffic accident, smash into a storefront, and set a building on fire.

c. He gets Sheeni's classmate to slip her sleeping pills so she falls asleep in class and gets expelled from boarding school.

d. He blames it all on "Francois."

Answer: d. Is there a shrink in the house?

Jennifer's Body 2009

Jennifer is an arrogant star cheerleader and Anita (a.k.a. "Needy") is a sensitive girl with a sweet boyfriend named Chip. Jennifer and Needy are total opposites, but were childhood friends and remain BFFs based on the fact that "sandbox love never dies." Then, one night, an aspiring indie rock band coaxes Jennifer into their van and uses her as satanic sacrifice. But the rocker boys think Jennifer's a virgin, like the ritual calls for. She's not, so instead of dying, she's transformed into a bloodthirsty demon on the hunt for teenage boy flesh.

When high school boys start turning up half-eaten, Needy discovers that Jennifer is to blame, but she's unable to stop her. Eventually, on the night of a school dance, Jennifer seduces Chip and lures him over to an abandoned pool house where she begins to feed on him. Needy finds them, and fights Jennifer off of her boyfriend, but gets bitten in the process. It ends up being too late for Chip, and he and Needy have their final goodbyes as he bleeds to death in the pool house. Later, Needy realizes that Jennifer's bite has turned her into a half demon herself. Tormented by Chip's death and fueled by her new demon status, Needy kills Jennifer and realizes she was never a very good friend after all.

LIFE LESSON

It's OK to remain in a harmful friendship with a selfish brat unless she eats your boyfriend. (Then, just kill her.)

Jennifer is a crappy friend to Needy because she:

a. Demands that Needy blow off her plans with her boyfriend to do whatever Jennifer wants.

b. Won't let Needy show off her cleavage because that's Jennifer's trademark look.

c. Flirts with any guy who seems interested in Needy.

d. Embarrasses Needy in front of her boyfriend.

Answer: All of the above. But, amazingly, Needy doesn't end the friendship until her boyfriend gets eaten.

Jennifer (Megan Fox), covered in Chip's blood and going after Needy.

SOUND BITE

NEEDY: You know what? You were never really a good friend. Even when we were little, you used to steal my toys and pour lemonade on my bed.

JENNIFER: And now, I'm eating your boyfriend. See? At least I'm consistent.

Fired Up!

Nick and Shawn only care about two things: football and girls. But the location of their summer football camp is moved from Daytona, a chick hotspot, to El Paso, a total sausage-fest. Then they learn that their high school cheerleading squad, The Tigers, is leaving for cheer camp during that same time. More interested in hooking up than playing ball, the duo ditches football camp and instead joins the The Tigers at cheer camp—where there will be plenty of cheerleading hotties to pounce on.

To their surprise, the guys accidentally fall in love with cheering—and Shawn really falls in love with the quick-witted cheer captain, Carly. But, when the squad finds out that Shawn and Nick have been planning to take off right before the big cheer competition for a party at home with their football buddies, the boys are told to leave. They go home, but they quickly realize that in the two weeks of camp, they've gone from football jocks to bona fide cheer dudes. They speed back to camp, throw on their cute black and orange cheer uniforms, and join the team just in time to jump, kick, and reverse cartwheel their way through the big cheer competition.

LIFE LESSON

A few weeks at cheer camp will turn big, horny football players into dedicated, sensitive cheerleaders.

With the boys on the squad, The Tigers:

a. Win the big competition.

b. Come in second place.

c. Come in third place.

d. Come in 19th place. They may be hot, but The Tigers can't cheer.

Answer: d. But that's 10 places higher than they came in the year before.

Nick (Eric Christian Olsen) and Shawn (Nicholas D'Agosto) have just arrived at cheer camp, though they are not exactly looking the part yet.

Easy A 2010

No one at school knows who Olive is until she lies to her best friend, Rhiannon, about spending a passionate weekend with a community college guy simply to avoid hanging out with Rhiannon and her weird nudist parents. When the lie spreads around school, Olive realizes she kind of likes being a topic of conversation. Then a gay friend begs her to extend her little white lie to include a night of sex with him so he'll stop getting bullied. Olive agrees and suddenly finds herself in the reputation-saving business: All of the outcasts and nerds in school begin paying her to lie about hooking up with them to make them seem cooler. When the judgmental kids at school start to call her names, she begins wearing a red letter "A" (for "adultery," from the book *The Scarlet Letter*) to mock them.

Soon, however, Olive is being harassed by hoards of horny high school boys, and she starts becoming disgusted with the entire male population. That's when her handsome childhood friend Todd confesses that he doesn't believe the rumors, and in fact, likes her. With his help, Olive performs a sexy dance number at a pep rally to get everyone to watch a webcast in which she confesses the truth to everyone. She becomes an instant web sensation and she even gets a new boyfriend.

LIFE LESSON

When your reputation needs a boost, pretend to be easy. When that gets old, tell everyone you were lying and score a new boyfriend while you're at it.

OLIVE: Whatever happened to chivalry? Does it only exist in '80s movies? I want John Cusack holding a boombox outside my window. I wanna ride off on a lawnmower with Patrick Dempsey. I want Jake from *Sixteen Candles* waiting outside the church for me. I want Judd Nelson thrusting his fist into the air because he knows he got me. Just once I want my life to be like an '80s movie, preferably one with a really awesome musical number for no apparent reason. But no, no, John Hughes did not direct my life.

Olive (Emma Stone) walks proudly through the halls wearing an "A" on her clothes as a symbol of her (fake) promiscuity.

For which of the following does Olive trade fake sex?

a. A $100 gift card to Best Buy.

b. A $50 gift card to TJ Max.

c. A $90 gift card to Panda Express.

d. Movie passes worth $40.

e. One coupon for 20 percent off at Bath & Body Works.

Answer: All of the above. Fake sex isn't worth what it used to be.

ABOUT THE AUTHOR

Nikki Roddy is a freelance writer based in San Francisco. She writes on culture, fashion, and music, and her work has been seen in both print and online publications, including *944 Magazine* and Bandega.com. She is the author of *Take Me With You: Off-to-College Advice from One Chick to Another*. In her off time, she enjoys reading, writing, watching movies, listening to music, and lounging in Dolores Park on sunny days. Visit her online at www.nikkiroddy.com.

AUTHOR ACKNOWLEDGMENTS

Thanks to Hallie Warshaw for giving me this amazing opportunity; to Karen Macklin for your support and insight; to Tanya Napier for your genius art direction; to Pam McElroy for keeping me on schedule and for keeping me sane (ya id!); to Deborah Brosseau for your hard work and encouragement; to The Teen Advisory Board for all of your thoughtful input and hilarious comments; to my family for being the funniest group of crazies I know—I couldn't do anything without your endless love and support; to Jeff Horn for always being there for me, never complaining about the last six months of our lives being dominated by teen movies, and for telling me that I should include *Lucas* in this book; to Sarah Jones and Kelsey Boxerman for being the best friends I could ever ask for; to Jennifer Cotterill and Sara Lyons for inspiring me every day with your creativity and general awesomeness; to the rest of my friends for your love and support; to everyone at A Fine Mess for always encouraging me to keep writing; and to John Hughes for making my favorite teen movies ever.

OTHER ZEST BOOKS

Reel Culture
50 Classic Movies You Should Know About
(So You Can Impress Your Friends)
by Mimi O'Connor

Scandalous!
50 Shocking Events You Should Know About
(So You Can Impress Your Friends)
by Hallie Fryd

47 Things You Can Do For the Environment
by Lexi Petronis with Environmental Consultant Jill Buck,
Founder of the Go Green Initiative

97 Things to Do Before You Finish High School
by Steven Jenkins and Erika Stalder

87 Ways to Throw a Killer Party
by Melissa Daly

The Look Book
50 Iconic Beauties and How to Achieve Their Signature Styles
by Erika Stalder

Off the Bus and On the Record
22 Candid Rock Interviews by the Teen Jouralists of
The Rock Star Stories
by Amanda Rich, Brittany Rich, Jaime Rich, and Zac Rich,
edited by Aaron Burgess

Crap
How to Deal with Annoying Teachers, Bosses, Backstabbers, and Other Stuff that Stinks
by Erin Elisabeth Conley, Karen Macklin, and Jake Miller

Take Me With You
Off-to-College Advice from One Chick to Another
by Nikki Roddy